HODDER HOME LEARNING

Better Maths

AGE 7-9

Rhona Whiteford and Jim Fitzsimmons

Illustrated by Sascha Lipscomb

As a parent, your encouragement and involvement can make an important contribution to your child's education. This book is designed to help your child build on the Maths skills that they have learned at infant school. It will help your child to learn and apply the rules of addition, subtraction, multiplication and division. There are also exercises on weighing, measuring, volume, shape and telling the time. There are four tests to help assess your child's progress.

How to help your child

- Keep sessions short and regular. A short period of work every day is usually more effective than a long session once a week.
- Build your child's confidence by offering lots of praise and encouragement. Rather than simply pointing out that an answer is wrong, you could say, 'You were almost right. Let's try again together!'
- Discussion is a vital part of the learning process for Maths, so do talk through the exercises.
- Don't treat the tests too formally. They are designed to make your child aware of their progress and give them a sense of achievement. You could keep a running total of their results separately and use this to encourage your child.

Hodder Children's Books

Easy addition

How quickly can you do this exercise?
Time yourself.

15 plus 10 = ☐ 29 plus 10 = ☐ 38 + 10 = ☐

21 + *five* = ☐ 32 plus 5 = ☐ 91 plus *five* = ☐

Write these numbers in words:

62 ▶ ☐ 28 ▶ ☐

23 ▶ ☐ 45 ▶ ☐

This took me ☐ minutes and ☐ seconds

Now do these. Add the units first and then the tens.

Tens Units	T U	T U	T U	T U
1 0	2 3	5 2	2 6	3 2
+ 2 6	+ 1 4	+ 1 4	+ 2 1	+ 3 4
☐	☐	☐	☐	☐

Problems Add up the cost of these items as shown:

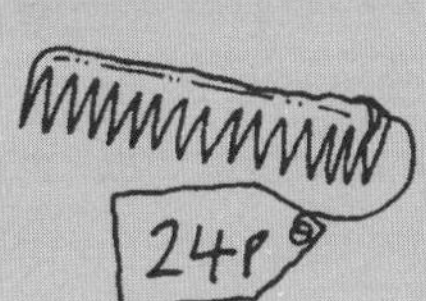

pen 45p	comb --------	pad ---------	pen ---------	comb ---------
comb 24p +	pad --------+	ball ---------+	ball ---------+	ball ---------+
69p	☐	☐	☐	☐

Addition with carrying

When the total **units** add up to 10 or more, each whole 10 is carried over into the tens column and added to that total.

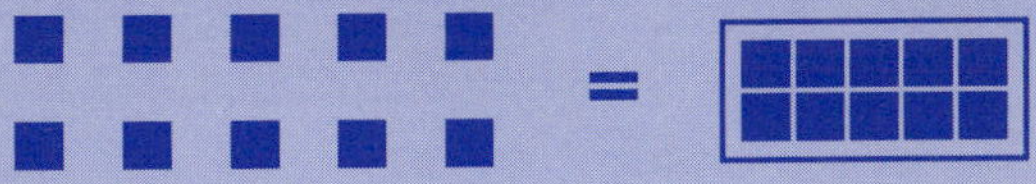

e.g.

16 + 26

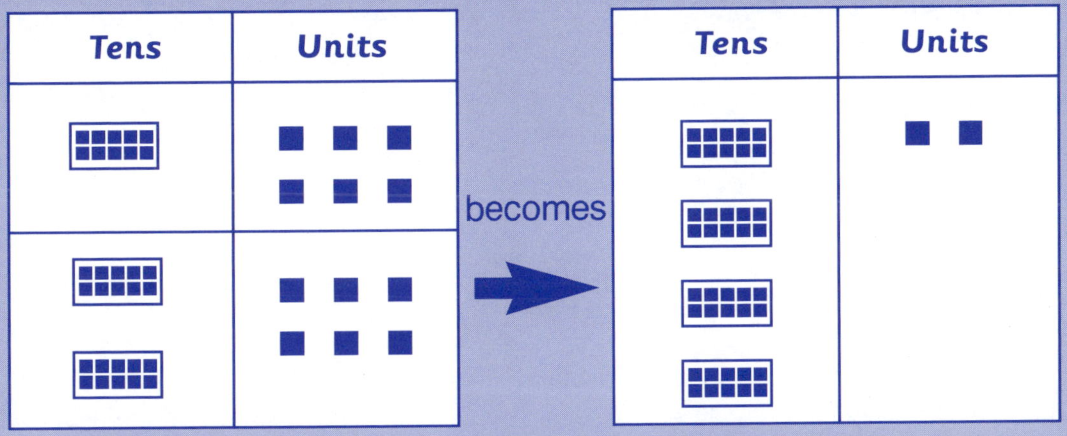

= 42

When writing the sum, we do the units first and say "6 plus 6 equals 12 so I can make one ten, which is carried over into the tens column, and place the 2 units in the answer space under the units column."

Carry the ten, writing it as 1 under the tens column.

T	U	
1	6	
2	6	+
4	2	
1		

There are now 4 tens in total

Try these sums:

T	U	
	9	
3	8	+

T	U	
6	1	
1	9	+

T	U	
1	4	
2	7	+

T	U	
3	7	
2	7	+

Adding three numbers

Look carefully at the problem below:

The shaded fish have been caught and we need to add their numbers up (3, 8 and 7) to get the total score.

Try three different number bonds as quickly as you can.

Add 3 and 8 first — or — Add 7 and 8 first — or — Add 3 and 7 first

Add 3 and 8 first	Add 7 and 8 first	Add 3 and 7 first
3 + 8 + 7	3 + 8 + 7	3 + 8 + 7
= ☐ + 7	= ☐ + 3	= ☐ + 8
= ☐ **in total**	= ☐ **in total**	= ☐ **in total**

What was the total in each case? ☐

Now do the same for this sum: add 6 and 4 and 5.

6 + 4 + 5	6 + 4 + 5	6 + 4 + 5
= ☐ + 5	= ☐ + 4	= ☐ + 6
= ☐ **in total**	= ☐ **in total**	= ☐ **in total**

Use the same problem solving method to do these:

T U	T U	T U	T U	T U
3 6	4 5	2 4	4 6	3 9
2 9 +	2 3 +	1 6 +	1 8 +	1 3 +
4 1	1 8	2 5	3 1	2 6
☐	☐	☐	☐	☐

Find the sum of the smallest three numbers below:

36 **92** **13** **21**

11 **16** **20**

T U

☐

Adding large numbers

10 tens make 1 hundred

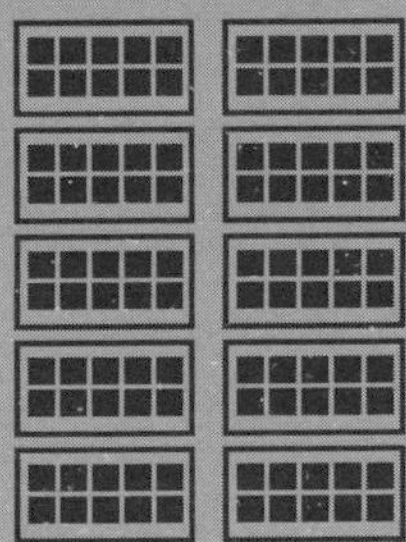

Write out this number in figures.

Hundreds	Tens	Units

1	0	0

H	T	U

How many hundreds,tens and units are in these numbers? (Try cutting straws into lengths and binding them in groups of ten with a rubber band to help you.)

143 = ☐ hundreds ☐ tens ☐ units

184 = ☐ hundreds ☐ tens ☐ units

Addition with carrying

When the total number of tens add up to 10 or more, each set of 10 tens is carried over into the hundreds column and added to that total.

e.g.

	H	T	U
121			
+ 293	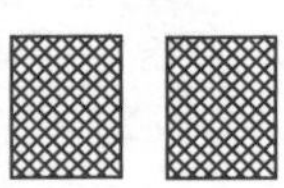		

becomes

H	T	U

4	1	4

= 414

The answer is 414. This is written four hundred and fourteen.
We write the sum like this:

Carry the new hundred over and write it under the hundred column.

H	T	U	
1	2	1	
2	9	3	+
4	1	4	
1			

TEST 1

❶ 29 + 6 + 13 = ☐

❷ 18 + 15 + 9 = ☐

❸ 22 + 6 + 30 = ☐

❹
```
 T  U
 2  8
 5  3 +
 ----
 [  ]
 ----
```

❺
```
 T  U
 3  0
 2  8 +
 ----
 [  ]
 ----
```

❻
```
 T  U
 5  6
 1  5 +
 ----
 [  ]
 ----
```

❼
```
 H  T  U
    6  7
 2  8  0 +
 -------
 [     ]
 -------
```

❽
```
 H  T  U
    3  2
    8  2 +
 -------
 [     ]
 -------
```

❾
```
 H  T  U
 3  6  0
    9  1 +
 -------
 [     ]
 -------
```

❿ If I scored 30 points on my game and my friend got 25 more than me, what did he score? ☐ (2 marks)

⓫ If I got 25p from Dad, the same from Mum and 40p from Gran, how much money did I get altogether? ☐ (2 marks)

⓬ My class has 30 children, class 3 has 38 children and class 4 has 20 children. How many children are there in total? ☐ (2 marks)

SCORE

/15

Subtracting tens and units

To do these calculations, work out the units first, then the tens. How quickly can you do them?

T U	T U	T U	T U	T U
4 7	3 8	3 8	9 2	7 3
1 6 -	1 5 -	2 4 -	5 1 -	5 1 -

This took me ☐ minutes and ☐ seconds

Exchanging

Sometimes we need to exchange a ten to be able to do the sum. This is like exchanging a large coin for several smaller ones.

e.g.

T	U
3	2
1	8 -

Look at the units.
We can't subtract 8 from 2
so we exchange one of the
top tens for units and
put it back in the units column.

We write it like this:

and say "exchange a ten and put it in to units in the unit column. So 12 units minus 8 units is 4 units. 2 tens minus 1 ten leaves 1 ten."

T	U
~~3~~ 2	[1]2
1	8 -
1	4

This is what we have done:

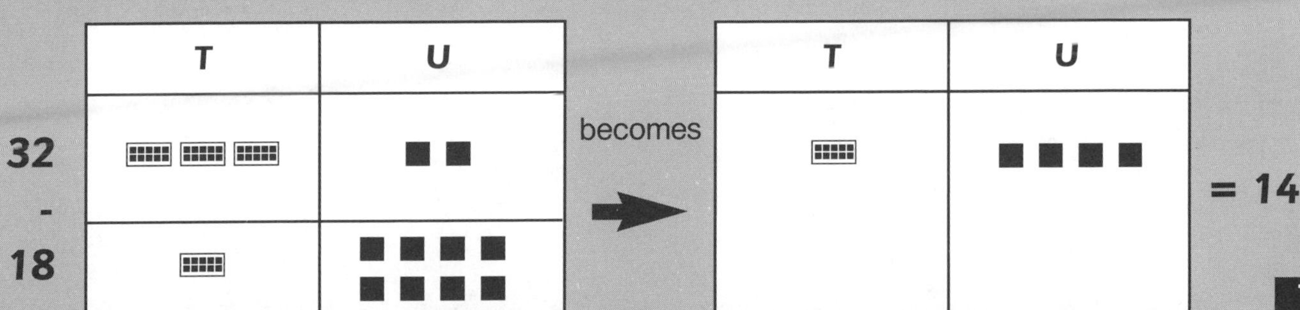

More subtraction

Exchange a ten to help you do these sums:

T U	T U	T U	T U	T U
8 2	5 0	5 3	8 1	5 6
1 4 -	8 -	2 9 -	1 7 -	3 9 -

Make three sums from these numbers. Remember the largest number goes at the top of the sum:

11 **19** **29**
59 **38**
46 **27** **42**
84 **13**

T U	T U	T U
-	-	-

Problems

1. Grandad is 75 years old but Gran is 9 years younger. How old is she?

T U

\-

2. The bus had 62 seats and 24 people were seated. How many empty seats were there?

T U

\-

3. There were 83 people in the Marathon. 38 of them were women. How many men were there?

T U

\-

4. It was a journey of 75 kilometres and they had travelled 46 kilometres so far. How many kilometres did they still have to go?

T U

\-

Subtracting large numbers

This is a straightforward subtraction sum. There were 329 children in school and 114 were boys. How many were girls?

H	T	U	
3	2	9	
1	1	4	-

Sometimes we need to exchange a hundred or a ten to help us do the sum.

e.g.

H	T	U	
4	1	5	
	5	4	-

We write it like this:

H	T	U	
~~4~~ 3	11	5	
	5	4	-
3	6	1	

415

-

54

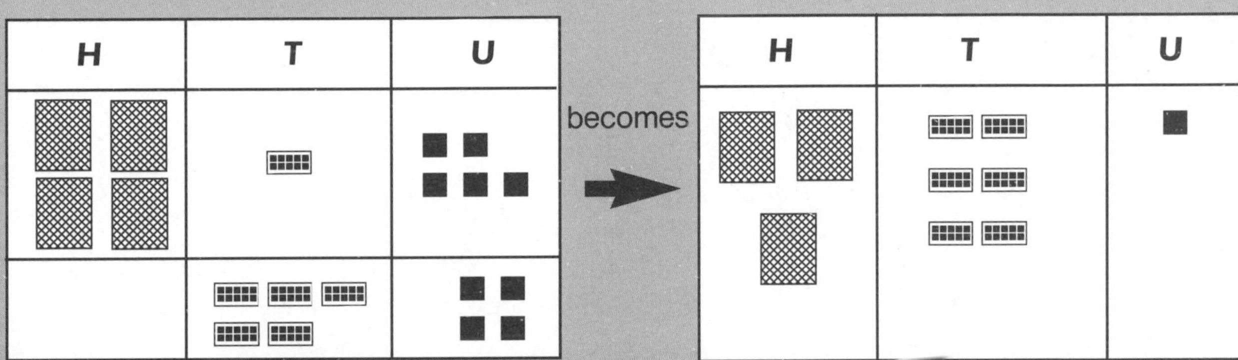

= 361

Now try these yourself:

H	T	U	
5	2	2	
	5	1	-

H	T	U	
3	2	3	
	4	1	-

H	T	U	
3	3	4	
2	8	3	-

H	T	U	
3	5	1	
1	9	1	-

H	T	U	
6	1	5	
	2	3	-

H	T	U	
2	6	8	
	6	9	-

H	T	U	
8	0	0	
5	6	0	-

H	T	U	
2	0	6	
	1	4	-

TEST 2

	❶	❷	❸	❹	❺
	T U	T U	T U	T U	T U
	3 4	9 6	8 3	4 1	7 5
	2 5 -	2 4 -	1 9 -	2 7 -	2 6 -

Make four subtraction sums from these numbers:

21 38 40
13 6
45 98 72
15 27

❻ T U -

❼ T U -

❽ T U -

❾ T U -

❿ Dave got 350 points in the competition and Sam got 26 less. How many points did Sam get?

H | T | U

⓫ The aeroplane holds 300 passengers. 46 can have window seats. How many can't?

H | T | U

⓬ There were 284 people on the train. 163 were women. How many were men?

H | T | U

(10, 11, 12 – 2 marks each)

SCORE

15

Multiplication

6 x 4 = 4 + 4 + 4 + 4 + 4 + 4 = 24

5 x 3 = 3 + 3 + 3 + 3 + 3 = 15

Fill in the missing numbers and work out the answers:

1. 2 x 5 = 5 + ____ = ____
2. 4 x 6 = ____ + ____ +____ + ____ = ____
3. 5 x 4 = ____ + ____ + ____ + ____ + ____ = ____
4. 3 x 9 = ____ + ____ + ____ = ____
5. 6 x 3 = ____
6. 7 x 2 = ____
7. 8 x 5 = ____
8. 6 x 6 = ____
9. 4 x 8 = ____
10. 7 x 4 = ____

We can set out multiplication sums in two ways:

3 x 6 = 18

- ***3 times 6 equals 18***

T	U
	6
x	3
1	8

- We write the 8 units in the units column of the answer space, and we write the 1 ten in the tens column of the answer space.

Try these:

T	U
	5
x	3

T	U
	7
x	4

T	U
	6
x	2

T	U
	7
x	3

T	U
1	3
x	5
	5
1	

- When we multiply bigger numbers we always start by multiplying the units.
- In this sum 5 x 3 = 15. We write the 5 in the units column of the answer space and carry over one ten and write it in the tens column under the bottom line of the answer space.

T	U
1	3
x	5
6	5
1	

- Next we multiply the tens. 5 x 1 ten gives us 5 tens. We add the 1 ten we carried over, which gives us 6 tens. We write 6 in the tens column of the answer space, so the answer is 65.

More multiplication

Try these:

T	U
1	5
x	3

T	U
1	3
x	6

T	U
1	4
x	4

T	U
2	8
x	2

Complete these table squares by multiplying the numbers from the column below the X with those in the row on the right of the X. Put the answer in the square where they cross, e.g. **5 x 2 = 10.**

X	2	3	4
5	10		
6			

X	3	4	5
6			
7			

X	7	8	9
4			
5			

Multiplying hundreds, tens and units

Let's try the sum 123 x 6 as an example.

We start off by multiplying the units column. 6 x 3 = 18, this gives us 1 ten and 8 units. We write the 8 in the units column of the answer space but we carry over 1 ten as we did before.

H	T	U
1	2	3
x		6
		8
	1	

Now we multiply the tens. 6 x 2 tens gives us 12 tens, plus the 1 ten we carried over = 13 tens. 10 tens = 1 hundred, so we have 1 hundred and 3 tens. We write the 3 tens in the tens column and carry over the 1 hundred to the hundreds column.

H	T	U
1	2	3
x		6
	3	8
1	1	

Now we multiply the hundreds. 6 x 1 hundred = 6 hundred. Add the 1 hundred we carried over to give us 7 hundred. We write 7 in the hundred column of the answer space to give the answer 738.

H	T	U
1	2	3
x		6
7	3	8
1	1	

Try these:

H	T	U
2	2	5
x		3

H	T	U
2	8	6
x		2

H	T	U
1	4	3
x		4

H	T	U
1	3	2
x		6

H	T	U
1	2	3
x		5

H	T	U
3	8	7
x		2

H	T	U
1	5	6
x		2

H	T	U
1	6	4
x		3

Find the cost of the following:

3 cakes

2 ice creams

4 soft drinks

3 teas

Problems

1. A cupboard has 3 shelves and each shelf holds 27 books. How many books does the cupboard hold?

2. There are 4 minibuses going on a day trip. Each minibus holds 26 people. How many people go on the trip?

3. There are 123 rubber bands in one box. How many are there in 4 boxes?

Multiplication and division link

Here are 10 sweets

Shared equally among 2 people

We write $10 \div 2 = 5$. The above example shows 2 piles of 5 sweets which is the same as $2 \times 5 = 10$. So we can write $10 \div 2 = 5$ because $2 \times 5 = 10$.

Here are 20 marbles - share them equally among 4 people. Draw the marbles to show each share.

Shared equally among 4 people gives

Complete the following sums: e.g. **20 ÷ 4 = 5** because **4 x 5 = 20**.

1. 8 ÷ 4 = ☐ ***because* 4 x** ☐ **= 8**

2. 10 ÷ 2 = ☐ ***because* 2 x** ☐ **= 10**

3. 18 ÷ 3 = ☐ ***because* 3 x** ☐ **= 18**

4. 15 ÷ 3 = ☐

5. 12 ÷ 4 = ☐

6. 25 ÷ 5 = ☐

We can make another three sums from one equation, e.g. **3 x 6 = 18.**

6 x 3 = 18 **18 ÷ 6 = 3** **18 ÷ 3 = 6**

Make three new sums from each of these:

1. 4 x 5 = 20

2. 3 x 7 = 21

3. 6 x 5 = 30

Division

Equal sharing. We can set out sharing or division sums like this:

18 ÷ 3 = or **3)18**

Remembering our tables we ask "3 times what is 18?"
3 times 6 is 18 so we write:

18 ÷ 3 = 6 or **3)18** with **6** written above

So each share is 6.

Use your tables to help complete these sums:

1. **28 ÷ 4 =** ☐
2. **32 ÷ 8 =** ☐
3. **40 ÷ 10 =** ☐
4. **36 ÷ 6 =** ☐
5. **24 ÷ 4 =** ☐
6. **15 ÷ 3 =** ☐
7. **2)12** ☐
8. **5)30** ☐
9. **3)24** ☐
10. **2)18** ☐
11. **4)28** ☐
12. **4)16** ☐
13. **5)25** ☐
14. **3)27** ☐

Fill in the missing numbers – divide the numbers in the top row by the numbers on the left. The top number should go first in the sum. Fill the answer in where the row and column cross in the square.

e.g. **6 ÷ 2 = 3**

÷	6	12	18
2	3		
3		4	
6			

e.g. **8 ÷ 1 = 8**

÷	8	16	24
1	8		
2		8	
4			

×

Sharing with remainders

Sometimes when we are dividing into equal groups we are left with too few units to make another equal group. The ones left over are called the **remainder**.

We write **25 ÷ 6** like this: $6\overline{)25}$

We ask 6 times what is 25? 6 times 4 is 24.

So, we write 4 on top of the sum and write 24 underneath the 25.
Now take it away. This leaves 1.

So **25 ÷ 6 = 4 *remainder* 1**.

```
    4 r 1
6 | 25
    24
     1
```

Try these. Use your times tables to help you.

$6\overline{)19}$	$5\overline{)21}$	$4\overline{)17}$	$8\overline{)33}$
$7\overline{)30}$	$6\overline{)44}$	$8\overline{)42}$	$7\overline{)29}$

Dividing larger numbers

If we have 85 pens shared equally among 3 people, how many pens are there in each share?

```
    T U
    [  ]
3 | 85
```

8 tens shared equally among 3 gives 2 tens each because 3 times 2 tens is 6 tens.
3 times 3 tens is 9 tens which is too many.
So, write the 2 on top, as before, and the 6 under the 8.
8 tens take away 6 tens leaves 2 tens.
So, write 2 under the 6 and bring down the 5 units to make 25 units.

```
    2
3 | 8 5
    6
    2 5
```

25 units shared equally among 3 gives 8 units each because 3 times 8 units is 24 units. Write the 8 on the top and the 24 under the 25. 25 take away 24 leaves 1.
So, each share is 28 remainder 1.

```
    2 8
3 | 8 5
    6
    2 5
    2 4
      1
```

Try these. Show your workings under each sum.

1.
```
   2 6
3 | 7 9
    6
    1 9
    1 8
      1
```
26 remainder 1

2. 4 | 95

3. 3 | 84

4. 2 | 59

5. 7 | 85

6. 5 | 76

7. 4 | 65

8. 6 | 89

Problems

1. 26 cakes are shared equally among 5 children.
How many cakes will each child get?
How many cakes will be left over?

2. 5 bus tickets cost 85 pence.
How much does each bus ticket cost?

3. How many children can have 4 sweets out of a bag of 96 sweets?
How many are left over?

4. 3 comics cost 87 pence.
How much will one comic cost?

Fractions

A **fraction** is part of a whole. It may be a big part or it may be a small part.

Fractions are written like this: $\frac{1}{2}$ $\frac{2}{3}$ $\frac{3}{4}$ $\frac{4}{5}$ (numerator) / (denominator)

The bottom number of a fraction is called the **denominator**. This tells you how many equal parts the whole is divided into. The top number of a fraction is called the **numerator**. This tells you how many parts there are in the fraction.

If a whole is cut into 2 equal parts we call each of these equal parts one half.
A half is written like this: $\frac{1}{2}$

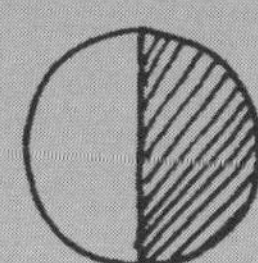

If the whole is cut into 4 equal parts we call each of these equal parts one quarter. A quarter is written like this: $\frac{1}{4}$

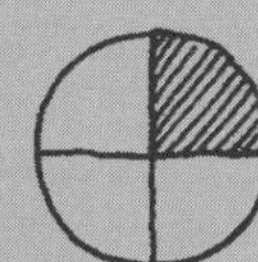

Here is a circle (a whole) divided into 4 equal parts.
3 of the 4 equal parts are shaded in, so the fraction is $\frac{3}{4}$

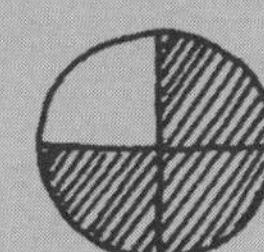

If a whole is divided into 3 equal parts, each part is one third. We write it like this: $\frac{1}{3}$

Colour in $\frac{1}{3}$

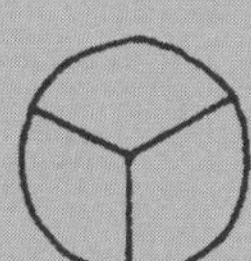

If a whole is divided into 6 equal parts, each part is one sixth. We write it like this: $\frac{1}{6}$

Colour in $\frac{2}{6}$

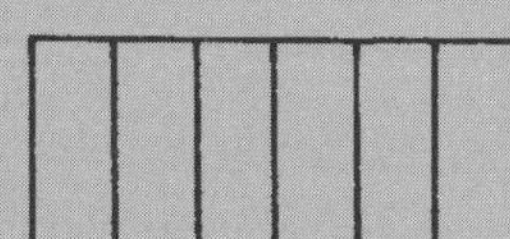

If a whole is divided into 5 equal parts, each part is one fifth. We write it like this: $\frac{1}{5}$

Colour in $\frac{3}{5}$

If a whole is divided into 10 equal parts, each part is one tenth. We write it like this: $\frac{1}{10}$

Colour in $\frac{6}{10}$

What fraction of these shapes is shaded in?

1. 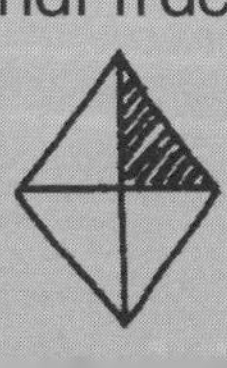

2. 

3. 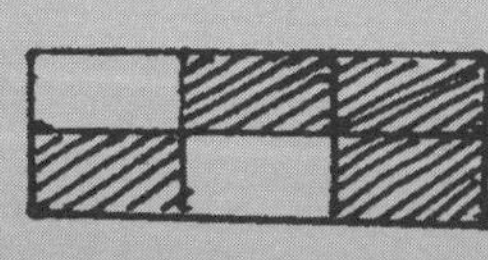

4. 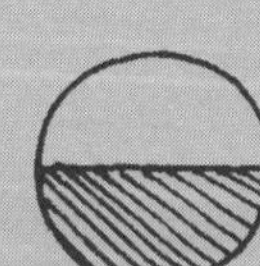

TEST 3

MULTIPLICATION

❶
T	U
	7
x	3

❷
T	U
1	6
x	2

❸
T	U
2	5
x	3

❹
H	T	U
1	4	3
x		4

❺
H	T	U
1	3	2
x		5

❻ *6 apples at 5p each =* ☐ *p*

❼ *3 oranges at 7p each =* ☐ *p*

❽ *8 bananas at 10p each =* ☐ *p*

DIVISION

❾ 6 ⟌ 37

❿ 5 ⟌ 27

⓫ 4 ⟌ 33

⓬ 3 ⟌ 77

⓭ 5 ⟌ 96

⓮ 4 ⟌ 73

⓯ If 47 marbles are shared equally among 3 children:
How many will each child get? ☐
How many are left over? ☐

⓰ 7 toffee bars cost 63 pence. How much does 1 toffee bar cost? ☐

FRACTIONS

⓱ Colour in $\frac{3}{4}$

⓲ Colour in $\frac{5}{8}$

What fractions of these shapes are shaded?

⓳

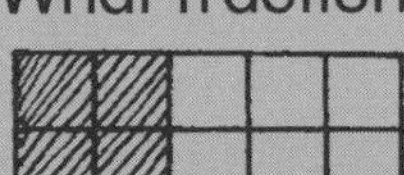

⓴

SCORE

/20

Weight

g is short for **grammes**.
kg is short for **kilogrammes**

1. How many 10g weights equal 100g?
2. How many 10g weights equal 50g?
3. How many 20g weights equal 100g?
4. How many 10g weights equal 20g?
5. How many 50g weights equal 100g?

Fill in the gaps with the right words - 'more than' or 'less than'

1. The jar of jam weighs ______ the pack of butter.
2. The cheese portion weighs ______ the jar of jam.
3. The pack of butter weighs ______ the beef stock cube.

Which item weighs the most?

Which item weighs the least?

The difference in weight between the portion of cheese and the pack of butter is 35g. We work this out by taking the lighter weight away from the heavier weight, e.g. 85g - 50g = 35g.

What is the difference in weight between:

1. The jar of jam and the beef stock cube? ______ g
2. The jar of jam and the portion of cheese? ______ g
3. The pack of butter and the stock cube? ______ g

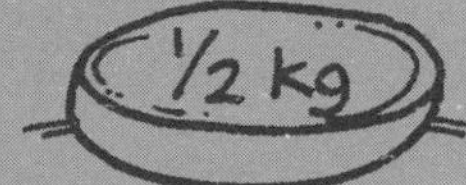

1000g = 1kg   500g = $\frac{1}{2}$ kg   250g = $\frac{1}{4}$ kg

1. How many 500g weights equal 1kg? ______
2. How many 100g weights equal 1kg? ______
3. How many 10g weights equal 1kg? ______
4. How many 50g weights equal 1kg? ______

This bag of sweets weighs 250g.

5. How many bags weigh 1kg? ______
6. How many bags weigh 500g? ______
7. How many bags weigh 1½ kg? ______
8. How many bags weigh 2kg? ______

Find the total weight in each box.

9. ______ kg ______ g   10. ______ kg ______ g   11. ______ kg ______ g

Change these weights into grammes.

12. 1kg 250g = ______ grammes

13. 2kg 127g = ______ grammes

Change these weights to kg and g.

14. 3450g = ______ kg ______ g

15. 1376g = ______ kg ______ g

Mr Smith weighs 110kg, Mrs Smith weighs 70kg, Johnny Smith weighs 40kg and Sally Smith weighs 35kg.

What is the total weight of the family?

16. 110kg + 70kg + 40kg + 35kg = ______ kg

Time

1. O'clock/ half past

What time do these clocks show?

Put the hands on to show the time.

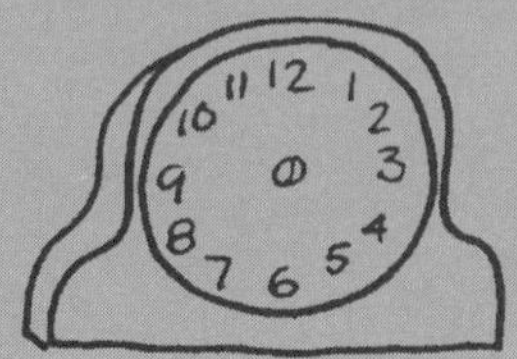

7 o'clock

$\frac{1}{2}$ past 2

2. Quarter to/quarter past

What time do these clocks show?

Put the hands on to show the time.

Quarter past four

$\frac{1}{4}$ to 9

3. Minutes

What time do these clocks show?

Put the hands on to show the time.

Twenty minutes to five

10 to 8

4. What time do these digital clocks show?

3:25	4:55	6:18

5. Fill in the numbers on these digital clocks to show the correct time.

:	:	:
Quarter to 8	twenty five minutes to 10	twelve minutes past 7

Times and dates

20 minutes past 9	can be written as	9.20
6.40	can be written as	20 minutes to 7

Write out these times:

1. 25 minutes past 3 can be written as

2. 10 minutes to 5 can be written as

3. 5.45 can be written as

4. 2.35 can be written as

Fill in the arrival times for these train journeys:

TRAIN LEAVES	JOURNEY TAKES	TRAIN ARRIVES
2 pm	20 minutes	
3.30 pm	45 minutes	
4.15 pm	30 minutes	
6.45 pm	45 minutes	

Use this calendar to help you answer the questions:

1. On which day did December begin?

2. What day does the 23rd fall on?

3. How many Tuesdays are there in December?

4. What day does Christmas day fall on?

5. What day is New Year's Eve?

Measurements

cm is short for **centimetre**

Measure the following using a centimetre ruler.

1. How long is your shoe? ______ cm
2. How wide is your book? ______ cm
3. How long is your pencil? ______ cm

There are 100cm in 1m (metre)

Measure out 1m on a piece of string and use the string to measure the height of the following:

<u>Height from the floor</u>	<u>Measurement in cm</u>
to the top of the table	cm
to the top of the chair	cm
to the bottom of the window	cm

Use a ruler to measure these lines in centimetres.

1. --------------------------------   2. -------------

3. ---

4. --

1. ______ cm   2. ______ cm   3. ______ cm   4. ______ cm

Draw lines of the following length:

1. 5 cm
2. 9 cm
3. 10 cm
4. 7 cm

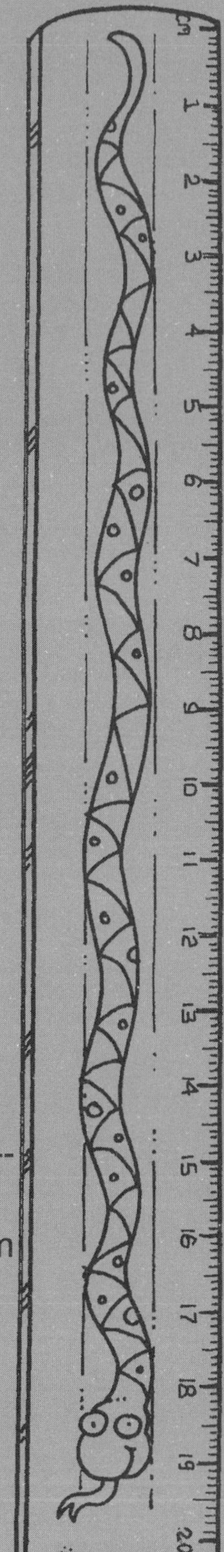

You can use this instead of a ruler.

100 centimetres = 1 metre 100cm = 1m

Change these lengths to centimetres.

1. 1m 45cm = ____ cm
2. 2m 25cm = ____ cm
3. ½m = ____ cm
4. ¼m = ____ cm
5. 3m 36cm = ____ cm
6. 1m 14cm = ____ cm

Change these lengths to metres and centimetres.

1. 155cm = ____ m ____ cm
2. 236cm = ____ m ____ cm
3. 334cm = ____ m ____ cm
4. 429cm = ____ m ____ cm
5. 105cm = ____ m ____ cm
6. 325cm = ____ m ____ cm

This chart shows Jon, Sam and Sally and their heights in centimetres.

1. How tall is Sam? ____ cm
2. How tall is Sally? ____ cm
3. How tall is Jon? ____ cm
4. How much taller is Sally than Jon? ____ cm
5. How much shorter than Sam is Jon? ____ cm
6. How much taller is Sally than Sam? ____ cm

If this rope was 1 metre long: 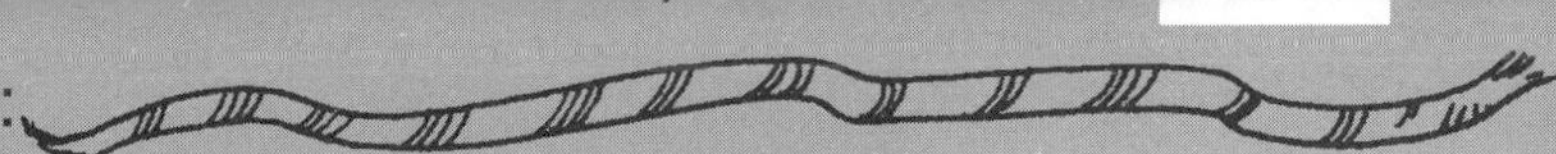

How many pieces 10cm long could be cut from it? ____

How many pieces 1cm long could be cut from it? ____

How many pieces 50cm long could be cut from it? ____

Shape

Right angles. These are corners which measure 90 degrees (90°).

Make one by folding a paper circle in half  and then in half again.
This is called a right angle. 

Use your paper to find the right angles in these flags. Mark them with a 

Squares and rectangles have 4 right angles. 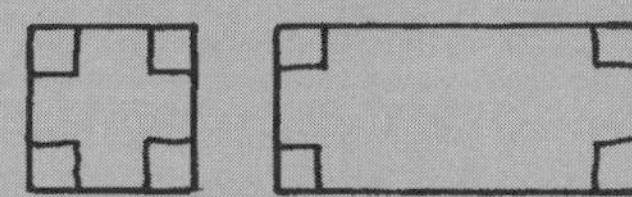

Join the dots to make 2 squares and 2 rectangles. Then mark the right angles in.

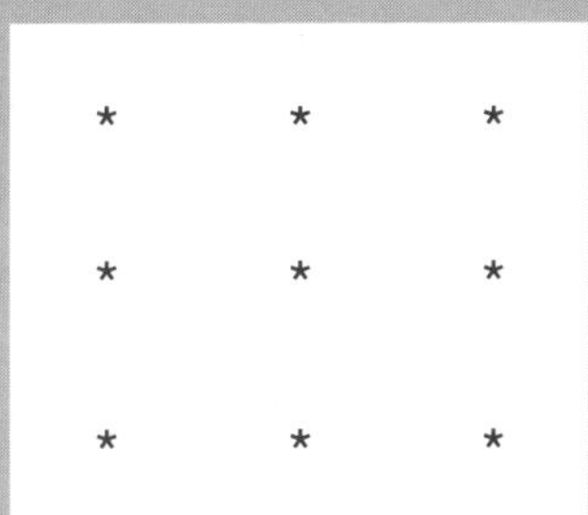

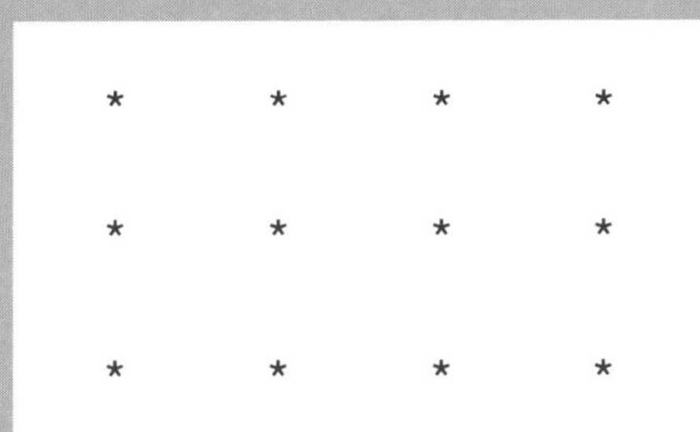

How many right angles are there along this line?

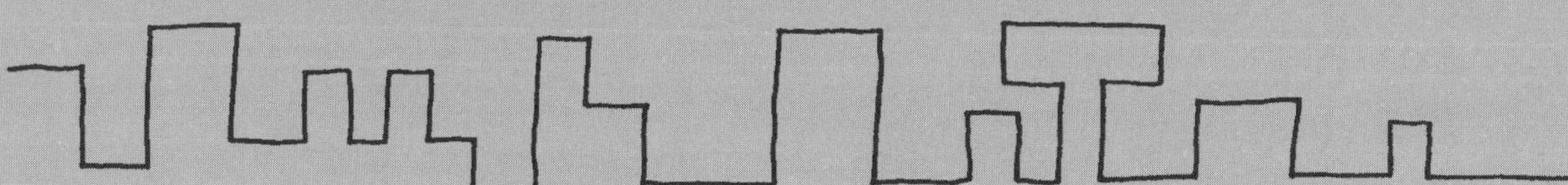

Make 3 triangles on these boards, each with one right angle.

Area

The **area** of some shapes is easy to calculate. It is measured in **square centimetres**. This is a square centimetre.

These shaded shapes are made up of whole square centimetres and half square centimetres. Count the area of each.

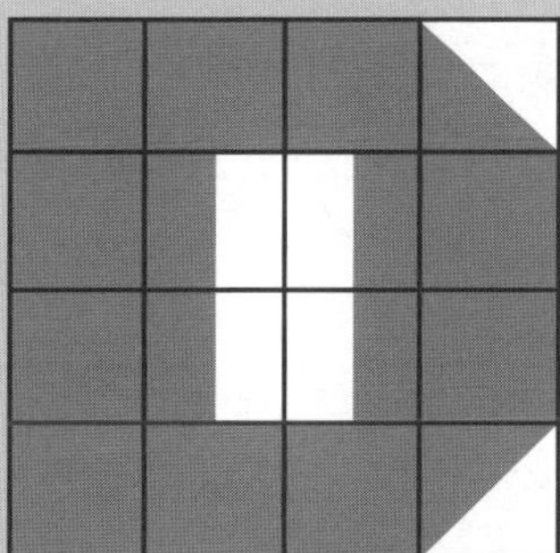

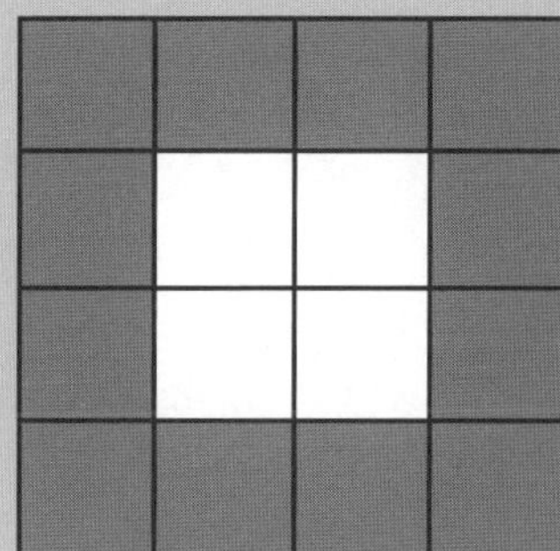

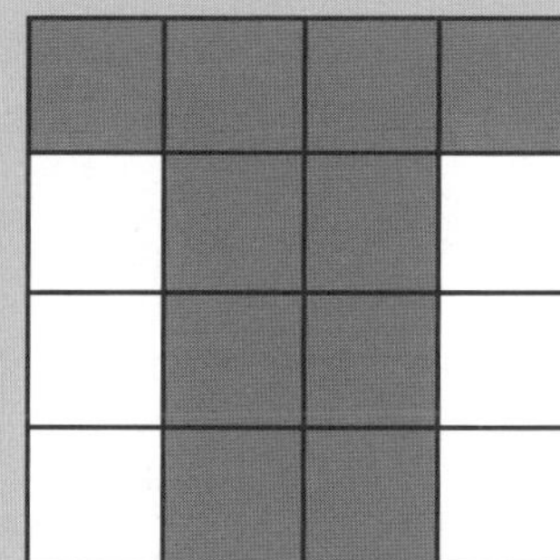

square cm square cm square cm

Irregular shapes. To find the area of these shapes you must decide how to count the small bits of a square. For example, can you add them together to make a whole square centimetre to add to the total square centimetres?

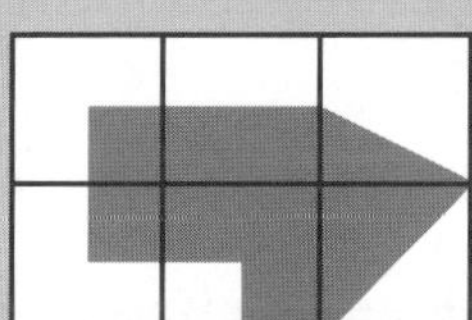

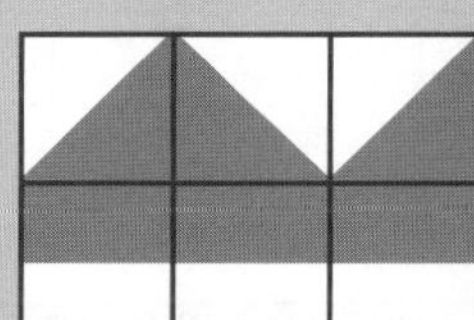

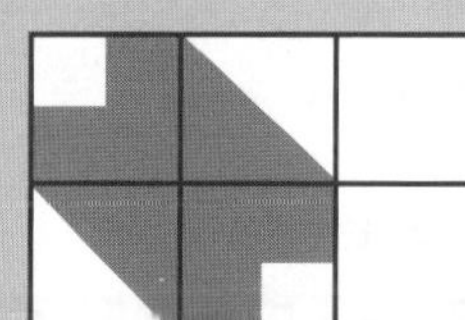

square cm square cm square cm

Draw 2 shapes in the grid below and write the area of each shape.

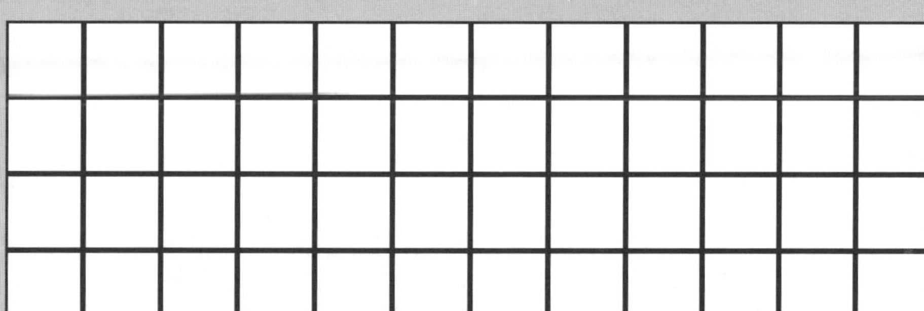

Capacity

Capacity is the amount a container will hold. We use the standard measures of millilitres and litres to measure liquids. 1000 millilitres (ml) = 1 litre (l)

Litres Find an empty plastic bottle that holds 1 litre. Then find these items:

large bottle washing-up bowl mixing bowl jug

Estimate how many litres of water you think each container will hold. Now measure the actual amount carefully, using your litre bottle. Record your findings below:

Container	Estimate	Measurement
bottle		
washing-up bowl		
mixing bowl		
jug/other		

Millilitres A medicine spoon holds 5ml at one end and 2.5ml at the other end. (If you don't have a medicine spoon, a teaspoon holds approximately 5ml.)

Find out what these small containers hold, using your spoon.

Container	Estimate	Measurement
Egg cup		
Dessert spoon		
Glass tumbler		
Thimble or other small container		

Reading labels

Find the following items in your kitchen. Now read the labels to see how much liquid each container can hold. Write the capacity of each item below:

Container	Capacity
Soft drink bottle	
Soft drink can	
Fruit juice carton	
Milk carton/bottle	
Washing-up liquid	

Volume

This is the amount of space taken up by a solid shape. Use building blocks like Lego or other cuboid or cube shapes to build these 3 shapes.

1. A tall thin shape of 30 blocks.

2. An irregular shape of 25 blocks.

3. A symmetrical shape of 36 blocks.

Make a cuboid shape with all your blocks.
Estimate its size. Now measure the following:

How long was it? ______ cm

How tall was it? ______ cm

How wide was it? ______ cm

TEST 4

MEASUREMENTS

Draw lines of the following length, starting from the dot below:

●→ ❶ 8 cm

●→ ❷ 6 cm

Measure this line.

❸ --

Change this length to centimetres.

❹ 2m 36cm = ____ cm

Change this length to metres and centimetres.

❺ 257cm= ____ m ____ cm

TIME

❶ What time does this clock show?

____

❷ Mark quarter to six on this clock

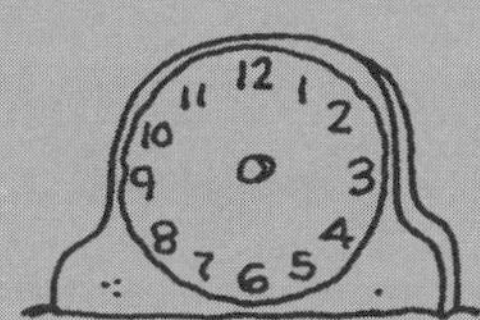

❸ What time does this clock show?

____

❹ 3.45 can be written as ____ minutes to ____

❺ A bus takes 2 hours and 40 minutes to complete its journey. If it leaves at 1 o'clock, what time will it arrive? ____

WEIGHT

❶ How many 10g weights equal 50g? ____

❷ How many 50g weights equal 100g? ____

❸ How many 250g weights equal 1kg? ____

❹ 1400g = ____ kg ____ g

❺ 1kg 750g = ____ g

AREA

Draw your initials on this cm square paper. What area is taken up by your initials? **(5 marks)**

CAPACITY

❶ How many ml in 2l? ______ ml

❷ How many ml does a teaspoon hold? ______ ml

❸ How many ml of liquid are there in your favourite soft drink can? ______ ml

❹ How many ml are there in half a litre? ______ ml

❺ How many ml does your shampoo bottle hold? ______ ml

SCORE

/20

Answers

Page 2
25, 39, 48, 26, 37, 96
sixty two   twenty eight
twenty three   forty five
36, 37, 66, 47, 66
54p, 44p, 59p, 38p

Page 3
47, 80, 41, 64

Page 4
11 + 7 = 18   15 + 3 = 18
10 + 8 = 18
10 + 5 = 15   11 + 4 = 15
9 + 6 = 15
106, 86, 65, 95, 78
40 (11, 16, 13)

Page 5
126 143
1 hundred, 4 tens, 3 units.
184, 1 hundred, 8 tens,
4 units.

TEST 1
1. 48   **2**. 42   **3**. 58
4. 81   **5**. 58   **6**. 71
7. 347   **8**. 114   **9**. 451
10. 55 points   **11**. 90p
12. 88 children

Page 7
31, 23, 14, 41, 22

Page 8
68, 42, 24, 64, 17
1.66 **2**.38 **3**.45 **4**.29km

Page 9
215, 471, 282, 51, 160,
592, 199, 240, 192

TEST 2
1. 9   **2**. 72
3. 64   **4**. 14
5. 49
6-9 Parent to judge answer.
10. 324 points
11. 254 passengers
12. 121 men

Page 11
1. 5 + 5 = 10
2. 6 + 6 + 6 + 6 = 24
3. 4 + 4 + 4 + 4 + 4 = 20
4. 9+ 9 + 9 = 27
5. 18 **6**. 14 **7**. 40 **8**. 36
9. 32 **10**. 28
15, 28, 12, 21

Page 12
45, 78, 56, 56
10, 15, 20
12, 18, 24
18, 24, 30
21, 28, 35
28, 32, 36
35, 40, 45

Page 13
675, 572, 572
792, 615, 774
312, 492
48p, 50p, 72p, 75p
1. 81 books **2**. 104 people
3. 492 bands

Page 14
1.2 **2**.5 **3**.6 **4**.5 **5**.3 **6**.5

Page 15
1.7   **2**.4   **3**.4   **4**.6
5.6   **6**.5   **7**.6   **8**.6
9.8   **10**.9   **11**.7   **12**.4
13.5   **14**.9

3, 6,9   8, 16, 24
2, 4, 6   4, 8, 12
1, 2, 3   2, 4, 6

Page 16
3r1   4r1   4r1   4r1
4r2   7r2   5r2   4r1

Page 17
1. 26r1   **2**. 23r3   **3**. 28
4. 29r1   **5**. 12r1   **6**.15r1
7. 16r1   **8**. 14r5
1. 5, 1   **2**. 17p
3. 24, 0   **4**. 29p

Page 18
1. $\frac{1}{4}$ **2**. $\frac{3}{8}$ **3**. $\frac{4}{6}$ **4**. $\frac{1}{2}$

TEST 3
1. 21   **2**. 32
3. 75   **4**. 572
5. 660   **6**. 30p
7. 21p   **8**. 80p
9. 6r1   **10**. 5r2
11. 8r1   **12**. 25r2
13. 19r1   **14**. 18r1
15. 15 with 2 left over.
16. 9p   **19**. $\frac{4}{10}$ **20**. $\frac{3}{5}$

Page 20
1.10 **2**.5 **3**.5 **4**.2 **5**.2
1. more **2**. less **3**. more
jam, beef stock cube
1. 90g **2**. 15g **3**. 40g

Page 21
1. 2 **2**. 10 **3**. 100 **4**. 20
5. 4 **6**. 2 **7**. 6 **8**. 8
9. 2kg 80g   **10**. 2kg 250g
11. 1kg 500g **12**. 1250g